Extreme Cuisine
Shocking Seafood

by Dinah Williams

Consultants:
David George Gordon, author of *The Eat-a-Bug Cookbook*
Andrew Zimmern, co-creator and host of *Bizarre Foods with Andrew Zimmern*

BEARPORT
PUBLISHING

New York, New York

Credits

Cover and Title Page, © Mike Veitch/Alamy; 4L, © Upperhall/Photolibrary; 4R, © Don Farrall/Photolibrary; 5, © Greg Elms/Lonely Planet Images; 6L, © Juniors Bildarchiv/Alamy; 6R, © Crista Thor; 7, © Miklas Njor/drr.net; 8, © Doug Wechsler; 9, © Michael Freeman/Corbis; 10L, © Paul Nicklen/NGS/Getty Images; 10R, © Sigurdór Guðmundsson; 11, © Pierre-Yves Jeanneret; 12, © Don Farrall/Photolibrary; 13, © Anna Lee; 14, © J.Garcia/photocuisine/Corbis; 15, © Mark Follon/Food & Drink photos; 16, © Bioquatic Photo; 17, © Markel Redondo/drr.net; 18, © George Grall/Getty Images; 19, © Poisson d'Avril/photocuisine/Corbis; 20, © Jeff J. Mitchell/Getty Images; 21, © Leser, sucré salé/photocuisine/Corbis; 23TL, © Andre Seale/Image Quest Marine; 23TR, © Todd Patterson/Food & Drink photos; 23BL, © George Grall/Getty Images; 23BR, © Dario Sabljak/Shutterstock; 23Spot, © Dario Sabljak/Shutterstock; 24, © mashe/Shutterstock.

Publisher: Kenn Goin
Editorial Director: Adam Siegel
Creative Director: Spencer Brinker
Design: Debrah Kaiser
Photo Researcher: Lindsay Blatt

Library of Congress Cataloging-in-Publication Data

Williams, Dinah.
  Shocking seafood / by Dinah Williams ; consultants, David George Gordon, Andrew Zimmern.
      p. cm. — (Extreme cuisine)
  Includes bibliographical references and index.
  ISBN-13: 978-1-59716-761-1 (lib. binding)
  ISBN-10: 1-59716-761-4 (lib. binding)
  1. Cookery (Seafood)—Juvenile literature. 2. Cookery, International—Juvenile literature. I. Gordon, David George. II. Zimmern, Andrew. III. Title.

  TX747.W5556 2009
  641.6'92—dc22

                    2008035302

For more information, write to Bearport Publishing Company, Inc., 101 Fifth Avenue, Suite 6R, New York, New York 10003. Printed in the United States of America.

10 9 8 7 6 5 4 3 2 1

MENU

Sour Fish Head Soup

Fish are eaten all around the world. Before cooking them, people often cut off the heads and throw them away—but not in Vietnam! There, it's the heads that some people want. They use them to make soup. Cooks add onions, tomatoes, pineapple, spices, and fish sauce to give the soup a sour and sweet taste.

Not everyone likes fish heads in their soup. Yet the world, like the sea, is a big place. Seafood that's shocking to people in one country may be popular in another.

catfish

red snapper

Catfish and red snapper are often used to make sour fish head soup.

5

Stinky Herring

Who wants to eat food that stinks? People in Sweden do! They enjoy eating sour herring, a dish that smells like rotten eggs.

How is this unusual food made? First, herring is put in a barrel with salty water for around two months. Next, the fish is canned and stored. Gas from the souring fish makes the cans start to bulge. After about six months, the stinky herring, called *surströmming*, is ready to be served. It is often eaten with bread and potatoes. The fish smells so bad that the cans are usually opened outdoors.

herring

opening a can of surströmming

KALLAX

★★★★★

Surströmming

En god klass...

Some airlines do not allow passengers to bring *surströmming* on board. They are afraid the cans will explode during the flight when the air pressure changes.

Deadly Pufferfish

Some fish can kill other animals when they're swimming in the sea. A pufferfish, however, can kill a person when it's served on a plate! Parts of the animal, such as the liver, are full of deadly poison. In fact, the poison in one pufferfish can kill up to 30 people.

When prepared properly, the meat of a pufferfish is safe to eat. In Japan, it is considered a treat. Only chefs who are trained to remove the poisonous parts of the fish are allowed to serve the deadly animal. Even so, about 100 people are killed every year from eating pufferfish. It's truly a dish to die for.

pufferfish

To protect the Emperor of Japan, it is against the law to serve him pufferfish.

Rotten Shark Meat

Greenland sharks store urine-like chemicals in their bodies. In fact, they store so much of them that fresh shark meat is poisonous to eat. Yet people in Iceland have found a way to prepare it safely.

First, they bury large pieces of shark meat in a pit. They leave it there for about two months so that it can rot. Then they dig up the meat and hang it in a shack to dry out for a few more months. During this time, a brown crust forms on the outside. When the shark meat is ready to be served, the outside is cut off and the white meat is sliced into cubes. The dish, called *hakarl* (HOW-kurl), can now be eaten. Who says people don't like rotten food?

hakarl

Greenland shark

Greenland shark meat that is not properly prepared can cause people to vomit blood.

shark meat drying out in a shack

Live Octopus Arms

Need eight reasons to eat a baby octopus? How about its eight arms waving from the bowl? Some people in South Korea love the wiggling dish, called *sannakji*. To make it, a live baby octopus is chopped up and seasoned with sesame seeds and sesame oil.

Sannakji is tasty—but dangerous to eat. The octopus's arms are still moving when they're served. As a result, **suckers** on the arms can cause the octopus pieces to get stuck in a person's throat. Diners must chew well before swallowing so that they don't choke on the squirming food.

octopus

12

Dipping the octopus's arms in sesame oil helps keep them from sticking to a person's throat.

octopus arms

Jellied Eels

When pulled out of the River Thames in London, long snake-shaped eels hardly look like dinner. Yet the English have been eating jellied eels for hundreds of years. To make the dish, cooks boil the fish with vegetables and spices. Then **gelatin**, one of the main ingredients in Jell-O, is added. The gelatin turns the liquid that the eel is cooked in into jelly. The jiggly dish is sold in shops and on the streets of London. People eat it either hot or cold.

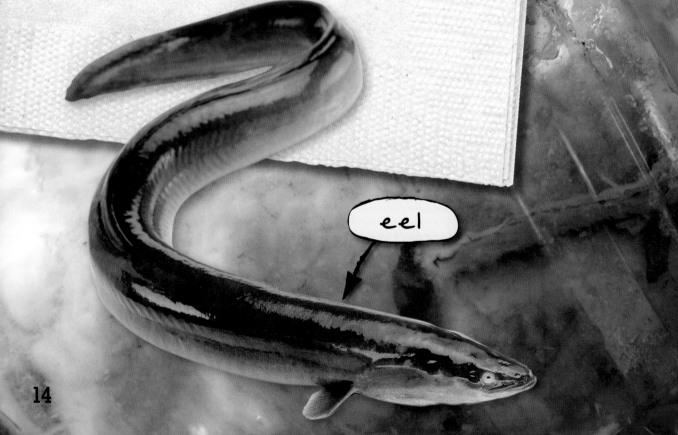

eel

jellied eel

When English soccer star David Beckham played in Spain, what did he miss most about England? That's right—jellied eels!

Boiled Sea Cucumbers

Don't be fooled by a sea cucumber's name—it's not a vegetable. Sea cucumbers are animals with leathery skin. They are covered with wart-like bumps and live on the ocean floor. In China, these cucumber-shaped animals are also a popular food.

A sea cucumber has little taste. However, its body easily soaks up the flavors and seasonings that are cooked with it. To prepare sea cucumbers, cooks must wash and boil them in salty water over several days. The meat can then be added to soups and stir-fry dishes. Why do people spend so much time preparing this food? Many believe that eating sea cucumbers can help treat health problems, such as high blood pressure.

sea cucumber

Sea cucumbers are very healthful to eat. They have more protein than almost any other food and they are very low in fat.

cooked sea cucumber

Sea Urchin

At first glance, a sea urchin looks too painful to eat. The outside of its body is covered with sharp **spines**. Yet inside each of these prickly sea creatures is a creamy treat— five pieces of *uni* (OO-nee).

Uni is the part of the sea urchin that makes the animal's eggs. It's a favorite food in Japan. The bright orange or yellow *uni* smells like flowers and feels like custard. It's eaten raw and melts on the tongue. Some people say there's a taste of the ocean in every bite.

sea urchin

Uni is the only part of a sea urchin that can be eaten.

uni inside a sea urchin

Cod Tongues

If cod could talk, they might ask why anyone would want to eat their tongues. Perhaps it is because they are so tasty.

Cod tongues were first eaten by poor people in Newfoundland—a large island in Canada. People cut the tongues out of fish heads that fishermen left on the **docks**. Over time, more and more people started eating them. Today, deep-fried cod tongues are found on the menus of many restaurants in Newfoundland, which shouldn't really surprise anyone. It's hard to stop a delicious dish from becoming a popular one as well.

cod

Long ago, there used to be a lot of cod in the Atlantic Ocean. However, fishermen caught so many of them that today Atlantic cod are in danger of dying out.

fried cod tongue

Where Are They Eaten?

Here are some of the places where the shocking seafood dishes in this book are eaten.

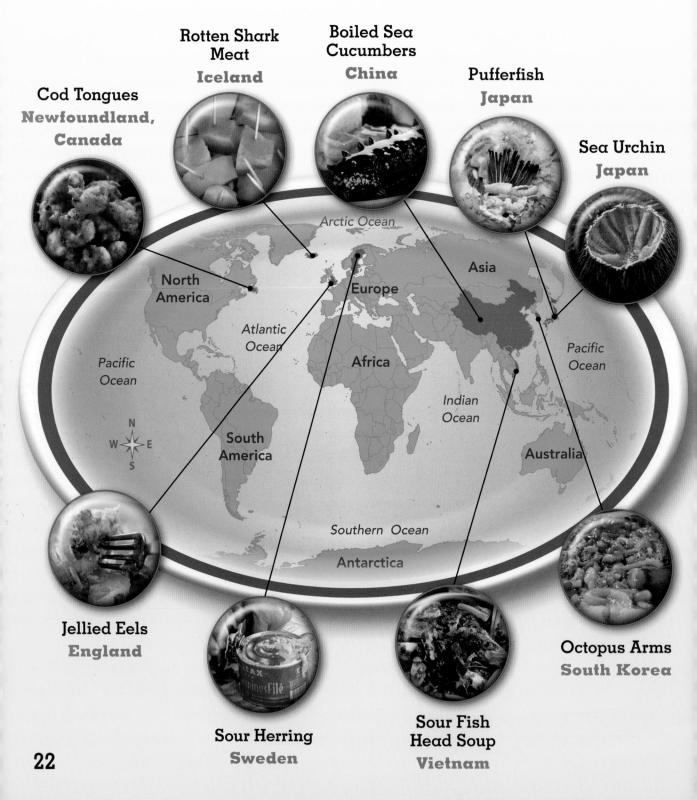

Cod Tongues
Newfoundland, Canada

Rotten Shark Meat
Iceland

Boiled Sea Cucumbers
China

Pufferfish
Japan

Sea Urchin
Japan

Jellied Eels
England

Sour Herring
Sweden

Sour Fish Head Soup
Vietnam

Octopus Arms
South Korea

Arctic Ocean

North America

Atlantic Ocean

Pacific Ocean

Europe

Africa

Asia

Indian Ocean

Pacific Ocean

South America

Australia

Southern Ocean

Antarctica

N W E S

Glossary

docks (DOKS)
landing areas where ships
load and unload goods

gelatin (JEL-uh-tuhn)
a cooking ingredient made
from animal bones and skin
that turns a liquid into a gel

spines (SPYENZ)
hard, sharp points
on an animal

suckers (SUHK-urz)
cup-shaped bumps on an
octopus's arms that help
the octopus hold on to food

Index

Bibliography

Hopkins, Jerry. *Extreme Cuisine: The Weird & Wonderful Foods That People Eat.* London: Bloomsbury (2004).

Schwabe, Calvin W. *Unmentionable Cuisine.* Charlottesville, VA: University Press of Virginia (1994).

Read More

Masoff, Joy. *Oh, Yuck!: The Encyclopedia of Everything Nasty.* New York: Workman (2000).

Rosenberg, Pam. *Eek!: Icky, Sticky, Gross Stuff in Your Food.* Mankato, MN: Child's World (2008).

Learn More Online

To learn more about shocking seafood dishes, visit **www.bearportpublishing.com/ExtremeCuisine**

About the Author

Dinah Williams has written and edited many books for children. She has also eaten many weird meals. She lives in Cranford, New Jersey.